Lil' MacDonald Likes to Hike!

A Rocky Mountain National Park Kid's Sing-Along & Hiking Guide

Jennifer Taylor Tormalehto

JOHNSON BOOKS
BOULDER

Lil' MacDonald went hiking, E-I-E-I-O!

On his hike he watches **Elk**, E-I-E-I-O!

With a BUGLE-BUGLE here, and a BUGLE-BUGLE there.

Here a BUGLE, there a BUGLE, everywhere a BUGLE-BUGLE.

Lil' MacDonald likes to hike, E-I-E-I-O!

Fun Facts: During the fall mating season, called the rut, bull elk challenge each other with loud bugling calls. The Shawnee name for elk is wapiti, which means "pale rump."

wooo-eeeee-arunf

Lil' MacDonald went hiking, E-I-E-I-O!

On his hike he notes **Coyotes**, E-I-E-I-O!

With a YIP-YIP here, and a YIP-YIP there.

Here a YIP, there a YIP, everywhere a YIP-YIP.

With a BUGLE-BUGLE here, and a BUGLE-BUGLE there.

Here a BUGLE, there a BUGLE, everywhere a BUGLE-BUGLE.

Lil' MacDonald likes to hike, E-I-E-I-O!

Aaaaaahhhhrrrruuuuuhhhhaaa Aaaaaahhhhrrrruuuuuhhhhaaa

Fun Facts: Coyotes "sing" to communicate with each other through yips, yelps, barks, and howls. Coyotes often travel alone but hunt in packs to catch larger prey.

Lil' MacDonald went hiking, E-I-E-I-O!

On his hike he hears an **Eagle**, E-I-E-I-O!

With a SCREE-SCREE here, and a SCREE-SCREE there.

Here a SCREE, there a SCREE, everywhere a SCREE-SCREE.

With a YIP-YIP here, and a YIP-YIP there.

With a BUGLE-BUGLE here, and a BUGLE-BUGLE there.

Here a BUGLE, there a BUGLE, everywhere a BUGLE-BUGLE.

Lil' MacDonald likes to hike, E-I-E-I-O!

Fun Facts: Bald eagles live near water and are experts at using their talons to catch fish, one of their main sources of food. Each year, bald eagle pairs return to build up their huge stick nests called eyries; the biggest one found weighed more than a pickup truck!

Lil' MacDonald went hiking, E-I-E-I-O!

On his hike he spots a **Black Bear**, E-I-E-I-O!

With a GROWL-GROWL here, and a GROWL-GROWL there.

Here a GROWL, there a GROWL, everywhere a GROWL-GROWL.

With a SCREE-SCREE here, and a SCREE-SCREE there.

With a YIP-YIP here, and a YIP-YIP there.

With a BUGLE-BUGLE here, and a BUGLE-BUGLE there.

Here a BUGLE, there a BUGLE, everywhere a BUGLE-BUGLE.

Lil' MacDonald likes to hike, E-I-E-I-O!

Fun Facts: The full moon in January is called the "Bear Moon" since black bear cubs are usually born that month. Bears are omnivores, meaning they eat both plants and animals.

Lil' MacDonald went hiking, E-I-E-I-O!

On his hike he seeks a **Squirrel**, E-I-E-I-O!

With a CHIP-CHIP here, and a CHIP-CHIP there.

Here a CHIP, there a CHIP, everywhere a CHIP-CHIP.

With a GROWL-GROWL here, and a GROWL-GROWL there.

With a SCREE-SCREE here, and a SCREE-SCREE there.

With a YIP-YIP here, and a YIP-YIP there.

With a BUGLE-BUGLE here, and a BUGLE-BUGLE there.

Here a BUGLE, there a BUGLE, everywhere a BUGLE-BUGLE.

Lil' MacDonald likes to hike, E-I-E-I-O!

Fun Facts: Chickarees are herbivores, meaning they eat only plants, and feed on pinecones. Animals store up "bad" yellow fat instead of "good" brown fat when they're fed people food. This can hurt the animal's chance of survival in winter, so please **"Don't Feed the Wildlife!"**

Lil' MacDonald went hiking, E-I-E-I-O!

On his hike he views a **Moose**, E-I-E-I-O!

With a BELLOW-BELLOW here, and a BELLOW-BELLOW there.

Here a BELLOW, there a BELLOW, everywhere a BELLOW-BELLOW.

With a CHIP-CHIP here, and a CHIP-CHIP there.

With a GROWL-GROWL here, and a GROWL-GROWL there.

With a SCREE-SCREE here, and a SCREE-SCREE there.

With a YIP-YIP here, and a YIP-YIP there.

With a BUGLE-BUGLE here, and a BUGLE-BUGLE there.

Here a BUGLE, there a BUGLE, everywhere a BUGLE-BUGLE.

Lil' MacDonald likes to hike, E-I-E-I-O!

Fun Facts: Moose are the largest animal in the deer family, weighing up to 1600 pounds (725 kg) and reaching 6.5 feet (2 m) in height. Moose are great swimmers, too!

Lil' MacDonald went hiking, E-I-E-I-O!

On his hike he beholds **Beavers**, E-I-E-I-O!

With a GNAW-GNAW here, and a GNAW-GNAW there.

Here a GNAW, there a GNAW, everywhere a GNAW-GNAW.

With a BELLOW-BELLOW here, and a BELLOW-BELLOW there.

With a CHIP-CHIP here, and a CHIP-CHIP there.

With a GROWL-GROWL here, and a GROWL-GROWL there.

With a SCREE-SCREE here, and a SCREE-SCREE there.

With a YIP-YIP here, and a YIP-YIP there.

With a BUGLE-BUGLE here, and a BUGLE-BUGLE there.

Here a BUGLE, there a BUGLE, everywhere a BUGLE-BUGLE.

Lil' MacDonald likes to hike, E-I-E-I-O!

Fun Facts: Beavers' front teeth never stop growing so they need to gnaw and chew often to keep their teeth worn down. Beavers remain active around their lodges year-round, even under ice.

Lil' MacDonald went hiking, E-I-E-I-O!

On his hike he spies a **Cougar**, E-I-E-I-O!

With a ROAR-ROAR here, and a ROAR-ROAR there.

Here a ROAR, there a ROAR, everywhere a ROAR-ROAR.

With a GNAW-GNAW here, and a GNAW-GNAW there.

With a BELLOW-BELLOW here, and a BELLOW-BELLOW there.

With a CHIP-CHIP here, and a CHIP-CHIP there.

With a GROWL-GROWL here, and a GROWL-GROWL there.

With a SCREE-SCREE here, and a SCREE-SCREE there.

With a YIP-YIP here, and a YIP-YIP there.

With a BUGLE-BUGLE here, and a BUGLE-BUGLE there.

Here a BUGLE, there a BUGLE, everywhere a BUGLE-BUGLE.

Lil' MacDonald likes to hike, E-I-E-I-O!

Fun Facts: Cougars have many different names—mountain lion, catamount, panther, puma—and they once roamed most of the United States. Cougars are carnivores, meaning they eat only animals.

Lil' MacDonald went hiking, E-I-E-I-O!

On his hike he sees **Bighorn Sheep**, E-I-E-I-O!

With a CRASH-CRASH here, and a CRASH-CRASH there.

Here a CRASH, there a CRASH, everywhere a CRASH-CRASH.

With a ROAR-ROAR here, and a ROAR-ROAR there.

With a GNAW-GNAW here, and a GNAW-GNAW there.

With a BELLOW-BELLOW here, and a BELLOW-BELLOW there.

With a CHIP-CHIP here, and a CHIP-CHIP there.

With a GROWL-GROWL here, and a GROWL-GROWL there.

With a SCREE-SCREE here, and a SCREE-SCREE there.

With a YIP-YIP here, and a YIP-YIP there.

With a BUGLE-BUGLE here, and a BUGLE-BUGLE there.

Here a BUGLE, there a BUGLE, everywhere a BUGLE-BUGLE.

Lil' MacDonald likes to hike, E-I-E-I-O!

Fun Facts: Bighorn sheep rams and ewes both have horns, which don't shed. During the autumn breeding season, rams charge one another and crash their horns together at speeds of 40 miles per hour (64 km/h)!

Lil' MacDonald went hiking, E-I-E-I-O!

On his hike he meets a **Marmot**, E-I-E-I-O!

With a WHISTLE-WHISTLE here, and a WHISTLE-WHISTLE there.

Here a WHISTLE, there a WHISTLE, everywhere a WHISTLE-WHISTLE.

With a CRASH-CRASH here, and a CRASH-CRASH there.

With a ROAR-ROAR here, and a ROAR-ROAR there.

With a GNAW-GNAW here, and a GNAW-GNAW there.

With a BELLOW-BELLOW here, and a BELLOW-BELLOW there.

With a CHIP-CHIP here, and a CHIP-CHIP there.

With a GROWL-GROWL here, and a GROWL-GROWL there.

With a SCREE-SCREE here, and a SCREE-SCREE there.

With a YIP-YIP here, and a YIP-YIP there.

With a BUGLE-BUGLE here, and a BUGLE-BUGLE there.

Here a BUGLE, there a BUGLE, everywhere a BUGLE-BUGLE.

Lil' MacDonald likes to hike, E-I-E-I-O!

wwhhiissttllee!!

Fun Facts: Yellow-bellied marmots, also called whistle pigs, make a whistling sound when they spot predators. Marmots survive the cold, subalpine winter by hibernating in their burrows from fall to spring.

Lil' MacDonald went hiking, E-I-E-I-O!

On his hike he regards **Ravens**, E-I-E-I-O!

With a QUORK-QUORK here, and a QUORK-QUORK there.

Here a QUORK, there a QUORK, everywhere a QUORK-QUORK.

With a WHISTLE-WHISTLE here, and a WHISTLE-WHISTLE there.

With a CRASH-CRASH here, and a CRASH-CRASH there.

With a ROAR-ROAR here, and a ROAR-ROAR there.

With a GNAW-GNAW here, and a GNAW-GNAW there.

With a BELLOW-BELLOW here, and a BELLOW-BELLOW there.

With a CHIP-CHIP here, and a CHIP-CHIP there.

With a GROWL-GROWL here, and a GROWL-GROWL there.

With a SCREE-SCREE here, and a SCREE-SCREE there.

With a YIP-YIP here, and a YIP-YIP there.

With a BUGLE-BUGLE here, and a BUGLE-BUGLE there.

Here a BUGLE, there a BUGLE, everywhere a BUGLE-BUGLE.

Lil' MacDonald likes to hike, E-I-E-I-O!

Fun Facts: Ravens are one of the smartest birds. Ravens bury food to eat later, drop food to break it open, and can trick other animals into giving up their food!

Lil' MacDonald went hiking, E-I-E-I-O!

On his hike he peeks at **Pikas**, E-I-E-I-O!

With a PHEE-PHEE here, and a PHEE-PHEE there.

Here a PHEE, there a PHEE, everywhere a PHEE-PHEE.

With a QUORK-QUORK here, and a QUORK-QUORK there.

With a WHISTLE-WHISTLE here, and a WHISTLE-WHISTLE there.

With a CRASH-CRASH here, and a CRASH-CRASH there.

With a ROAR-ROAR here, and a ROAR-ROAR there.

With a GNAW-GNAW here, and a GNAW-GNAW there.

With a BELLOW-BELLOW here, and a BELLOW-BELLOW there.

With a CHIP-CHIP here, and a CHIP-CHIP there.

With a GROWL-GROWL here, and a GROWL-GROWL there.

With a SCREE-SCREE here, and a SCREE-SCREE there.

With a YIP-YIP here, and a YIP-YIP there.

With a BUGLE-BUGLE here, and a BUGLE-BUGLE there.

Here a BUGLE, there a BUGLE, everywhere a BUGLE-BUGLE.

Lil' MacDonald likes to hike, E-I-E-I-O!

Fun Facts: During the summer, pikas store "haystacks" of alpine plants in their burrows, which they feed on all winter long. Pikas are sensitive to a warming climate in the alpine tundra.

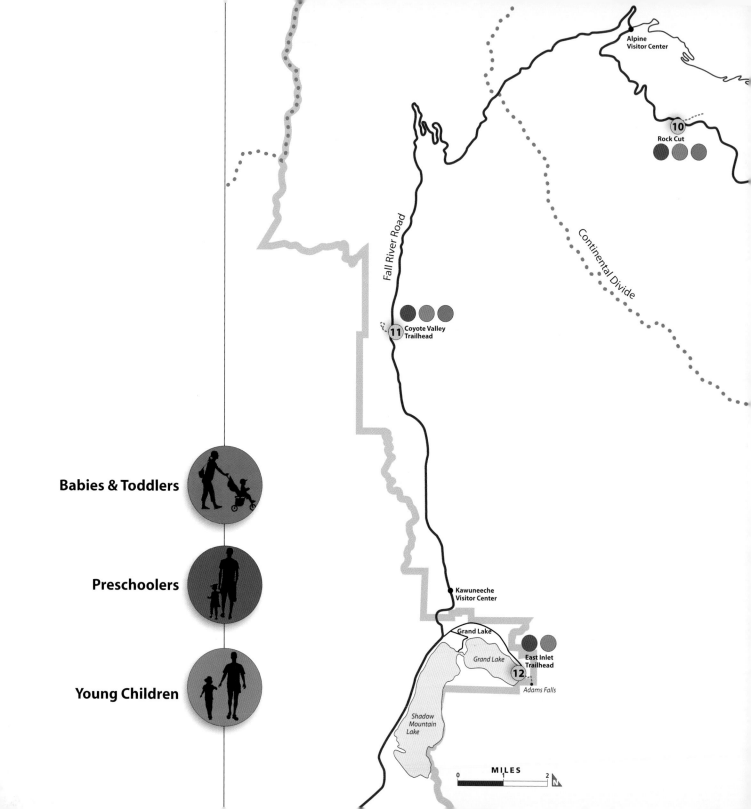

Alpine
Visitor Center

10
Rock Cut

Continental Divide

Fall River Road

11
Coyote Valley
Trailhead

Babies & Toddlers

Preschoolers

Young Children

Kawuneeche
Visitor Center

Grand Lake

Grand Lake

East Inlet
Trailhead

12

Adams Falls

*Shadow
Mountain
Lake*

MILES

0   1   2   N

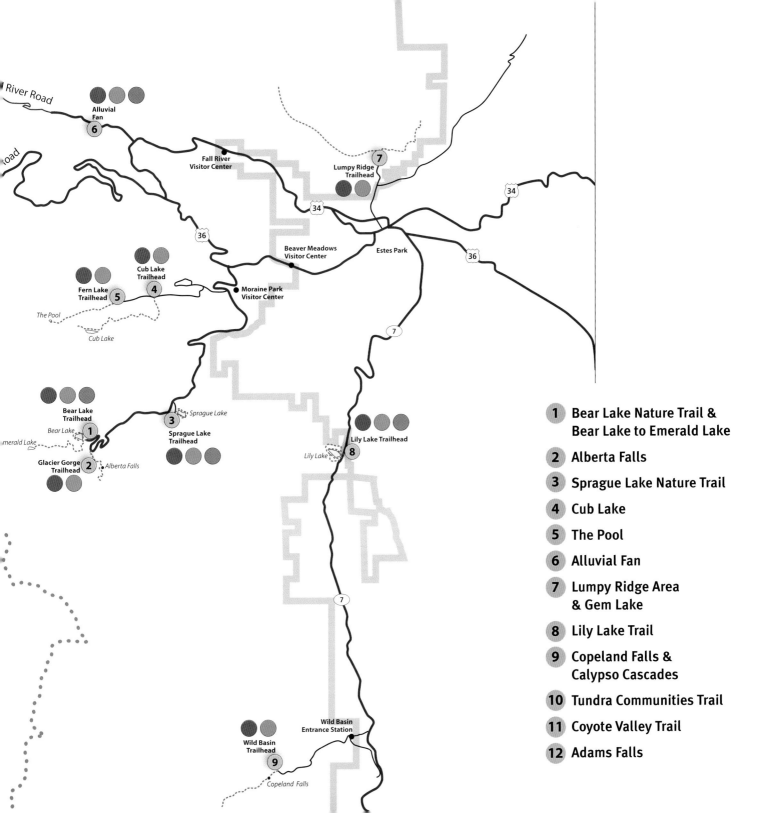

River Road

Alluvial Fan
6

Fall River
Visitor Center

Lumpy Ridge
Trailhead
7

34

34

36

Beaver Meadows
Visitor Center

Estes Park

Moraine Park
Visitor Center

36

Cub Lake
Trailhead
4

Fern Lake
Trailhead
5

The Pool

Cub Lake

7

Bear Lake
Trailhead
1

Sprague Lake

Bear Lake

Sprague Lake
Trailhead
3

emerald Lake

Glacier Gorge
Trailhead
2

Alberta Falls

Lily Lake Trailhead
8

Lily Lake

7

Wild Basin
Entrance Station

Wild Basin
Trailhead
9

Copeland Falls

1 Bear Lake Nature Trail &
Bear Lake to Emerald Lake

2 Alberta Falls

3 Sprague Lake Nature Trail

4 Cub Lake

5 The Pool

6 Alluvial Fan

7 Lumpy Ridge Area
& Gem Lake

8 Lily Lake Trail

9 Copeland Falls &
Calypso Cascades

10 Tundra Communities Trail

11 Coyote Valley Trail

12 Adams Falls

Top 12 Hikes for Tikes in Rocky Mountain National Park

The highlighted trails and destinations are great for families with babies in backpack carriers, some suitable for strollers, toddlers and young children on their first "big" hike. Take a stroll along a stream, walk to a wonderful waterfall, amble around a lake, and trek at the top of the tundra! There are also hikes from the Moraine Park, Alpine, and Kawuneeche Visitor Centers. For information on trail conditions, weather forecast, shuttle buses, etc., check out RMNP's website at www.nps.gov/romo or phone (970) 586-1206.

Leave No Trace — Enjoy & Care for Nature

Love the land and the plants and animals that call it home! By following these ideals we can all help to preserve the outdoors for future generations and protect wildlife.

- Plan ahead and be prepared
- Leave nature as you find it
- Don't litter and pack out trash
- Hike on trails and use established campsites only
- Be cautious with campfires
- Be considerate of other visitors
- Respect wildlife

Day Hike Equipment Checklist

Weather in the mountains can be warm and sunny one moment and cold and stormy the next, so make sure you're prepared by packing right. Check the weather forecast before you head out hiking and plan to be down below treeline early in the day to avoid thunderstorms. Drinking plenty of water is very important at higher altitudes. Drinking water is limited in the park and is available at visitor center restrooms (except Alpine Visitor Center); it's best to bring your own. Here's what's suggested for a happy hike:

Short day hikes

- Backpack
- Topographic Map & Compass
- Sturdy Hiking Boots or Hiking Shoes
- Wicking Shirt & Shorts/Pants
- 1-Liter Water Bottle (per person)
- Energy Snack Foods
- Sunscreen, Lip Balm, Sunglasses with UV Protection & Hat
- First-aid Kit & Insect Repellent
- Waterproof/Windproof Jacket & Pants
- Camera
- Trip Itinerary left with family or friends

Bear Lake Nature Trail and Bear Lake to Emerald Lake

1

Distance Round-trip:
Bear Lake Nature Trail 0.5 mile / 0.8 km
Bear Lake to Emerald Lake 3.6 miles / 5.8 km
Difficulty: easy to challenging

Bear Lake is a picturesque alpine lake surrounded by an evergreen forest with glimpses of the surrounding mountain peaks. The rolling trail around Bear Lake is very popular for all ages and is a great introduction to Rocky Mountain National Park. Strollers are welcome on the trail around Bear Lake, but not beyond. From the Bear Lake Trailhead there's also a superb trail that climbs to Nymph Lake, continues up to Dream Lake, and ends at Emerald Lake, with each of the lakes reflecting their names. At the trail's end, the views of the Continental Divide of the Rocky Mountains are truly magnificent!

2 Alberta Falls

Distance Round-trip: 1.6 miles / 2.6 km
Difficulty: easy to moderate

From the Glacier Gorge Trailhead, the trail up to Alberta Falls is a pleasant mix of aspens, evergreens, and the rushing water of Glacier Creek. Turn left at the T-junction and continue on the meandering trail uphill to the sign-posted falls. You can also hike to Alberta Falls from Bear Lake, which is only 0.2 mile farther. These beautiful falls are an extremely popular destination in the park and an enjoyable hike for families.

3 Sprague Lake Nature Trail

Distance Round-trip: 0.5 mile / 0.8 km
Difficulty: easy

  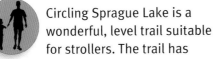

Circling Sprague Lake is a wonderful, level trail suitable for strollers. The trail has benches and decks to rest at and take in nature. There's abundant wildlife in and around this water oasis plus the Continental Divide pops into view in places. Picnic tables are available near the parking area to make for a perfect day in the park.

4 Cub Lake

Distance Round-trip: 4.6 miles / 7.4 km
Difficulty: moderate to challenging

  Start at the Cub Lake Trailhead and follow the Cub Lake Trail through Moraine Park as it curves west to follow Cub Creek. The rolling trail winds through the trees and eventually climbs uphill to Cub Lake. The lily pad–covered lake is exceptionally eye-catching and a good place to look for sometimes-seen moose!

5 The Pool

Distance Round-trip: 3.4 miles / 5.5 km
Difficulty: moderate to challenging

  This easygoing hike to The Pool, along the Fern Lake Trail, follows the Big Thompson River westward weaving through woodlands. The rushing river follows the trail to a bridge overlooking the blue-green whirling waters of The Pool. Take time to rest and refresh before enjoying the hike back.

6 Alluvial Fan

Distance Round-trip: 0.6 mile / 0.9 km
Difficulty: easy

This mellow, hard-packed trail connects two adjacent parking lots, with picnic areas, off of the Endovalley Road. The trail bridges the Roaring River and there are wonderful views of waterfalls and Horseshoe Park. The deposit of large boulders and sand is the result of a flood that happened here in 1982 when the remote Lawn Lake dam gave way. This hike is perfect for an easy family stroll with young children and is good for strollers, too.

7 Lumpy Ridge Area and Gem Lake

Distance Round-trip:
Lumpy Ridge Area 1.7 miles / 2.7 km
Gem Lake 3.4 miles / 5.5 km
Difficulty: moderate to challenging

  From the Lumpy Ridge Trailhead take the Twin Owls Black Canyon Trail over a knoll to a T-junction in the trail. Turn left and hike a short distance to see amazing views of the Continental Divide and Longs Peak. Double-back to the T-junction and continue eastward uphill to the Gem Lake Trail junction, turn right and hike downhill a half mile to the parking area. If your destination is Gem Lake, take the Gem Lake Trail from the parking lot and hike uphill half a mile and turn right at the trail T-junction. Continue hiking uphill another 1.2 miles (1.9 km) to reach the lake, which is sheltered by rock outcrops. Gem Lake is one of the park's jewels!

8 Lily Lake Trail

Distance Round-trip: 0.8 mile / 1.3 km
Difficulty: easy

The flat trail around Lily Lake offers benches, a fishing pier, an observation deck, a picnic area, and is stroller-friendly—fantastic for a family day of fun! Stunning mountains and rocky ridges surround Lily Lake giving it a quintessential alpine feel.

Copeland Falls and Calypso Cascades

9

Distance Round-trip:
Copeland Falls 0.6 mile / 1.0 km
Calypso Cascades 3.6 miles / 5.8 km
Difficulty: easy to challenging

Begin at the Wild Basin Trailhead for a gentle hike to reach the Upper and Lower Copeland Falls of the North St. Vrain Creek. There's the option to continue on up the trail that follows the creek another 1.5 miles (2.4 km) to enjoy Calypso Cascades from a wooden bridge.

10 Tundra Communities Trail

Distance Round-trip: 1.0 mile / 1.6 km
Difficulty: moderate

High on the alpine tundra, the Tundra Communities Trail starts at the Rock Cut parking lot, along Trail Ridge Road (12,050 ft/ 3673 m). Strollers are allowed on this paved but steep trail that climbs almost 200 feet (60 m) in half a mile to the Toll Memorial. Take in the stunning vistas of the surrounding mountains and tundra; it's worth the effort!

11 Coyote Valley Trail

Distance Round-trip: 1.0 mile / 1.6 km
Difficulty: easy

The stunning Kawuneeche Valley is the location of this level trail through gorgeous mountain meadow scenery with opportunities to see wildlife. Begin at the Coyote Valley Trailhead and cross the bridge over the Colorado River. A family-friendly trail for young children and strollers, this out-and-back trail loops at the end and has a picnic area just over the bridge.

12 Adams Falls

Distance Round-trip: 0.6 mile / 1.0 km
Difficulty: easy to moderate

  This very popular west side waterfall is easily accessed from the East Inlet Trailhead, near Grand Lake. Take a right at the loop trail intersection to the falls' overlook viewing platform. There's the option to follow the rest of the loop trail for another 1.0 mile (1.6 km) for a bit more challenge and to see some more pretty cascades.

History of Rocky Mountain National Park

Rocky Mountain National Park's alpine beauty is the result of major geologic events, especially the massive glaciers that carved and shaped its peaks, rivers, and meadows over tens of thousands of years. The rugged mountainous terrain of the park is accented with remnants of glaciers and permanent snowfields above treeline, which starts around 11,200 feet. The elevation of the park ranges from over 7700 feet in the valleys to 14,259 feet on the summit of Longs Peak. Longs Peak is named after Major Stephen H. Long who viewed the peak during an early scientific exploration to the Rocky Mountains in 1820.

When the glaciers of the last Ice Age began retreating about 11,000 years ago, the Clovis Paleo-Indians first traveled and hunted wooly mammoths in the area. Artifacts of arrowheads, spearheads and scrapers discovered in the park prove the prehistoric presence of people. Several American Indian tribes, mainly the Ute and Arapaho and for a shorter time the Apache, hunted and were seasonal residents in the area until the late 1800s. Due to the harsh winters at high elevations, the area was never a permanent settlement for any tribe.

The 1859 gold rush attracted thousands of people to the future state of Colorado. That fall, the first settler to see and then homestead on the east side of the park was Joel Estes and his family, who ranched in the area that is now Estes Park. Tourists started visiting Estes Park from the eastern half of the US and Europe. They were attracted by the area's superb mountain scenery and promoted health benefits

of the high-altitude air. In 1873, world adventurer and travel author Isabella Bird, a Victorian Englishwoman, was enamored with the beauty of Estes Park and wrote a fascinating account of her stay in her book, *A Lady's Life in the Rocky Mountains*.

By the end of the 1800s, there was a growing national movement to preserve our natural environment thanks to the vision and efforts of people like John Muir. Muir is considered to be a founder of the country's conservation movement. In 1872 the first national park, Yellowstone, was created. In 1889 Enos Mills, an Estes Park area naturalist and nature guide met John Muir by chance while visiting California. Their similar beliefs about the natural world led to a lifelong friendship and encouraged Mills to follow in Muir's footsteps to promote forming a national park in the Estes Park region.

In 1909, Enos Mills began his heartfelt and tireless campaign to create the nation's tenth national park. For the next six years, Mills wrote and published thousands of letters and articles, lectured across the country, and lobbied Congress about the benefits of a national park in the Rocky Mountains surrounding Estes Park. Mills truly believed "The wild gardens of Nature are the best kindergartens. The child who breathes the pure air among the pines, and plays among the birds and flowers, has the greatest of advantages."

On January 26, 1915, President Woodrow Wilson signed the act of Congress that would establish, preserve, and protect the now 415 square miles of Rocky Mountain National Park. On September 4th of that year, a dedication ceremony was held in the newly created national park with Enos Mills, the "Father of Rocky Mountain National Park," giving the keynote speech.

For Kai, with Love

*To Kai's cousins and all
children who cherish nature.*

MEET THE AUTHOR

Jennifer Taylor Tormalehto has been teaching middle school science in Colorado for over a decade. Her first book is a simple expression of her desire to share her love of nature and learning with children. She spends her free time with her family enjoying Rocky Mountain National Park and is grateful to live and teach in the beauty of Estes Park.

Published by Johnson Books, a Big Earth Publishing company
3360 Mitchell Lane, Suite E, Boulder, Colorado 80301
1-800-258-5830
E-mail: books@bigearthpublishing.com
www.bigearthpublishing.com

Editor: Mira Perrizo
Cover and text design: Rebecca Finkel

9 8 7 6 5 4 3 2 1

Printed in China by Four Colour Print Group